Bookmobile
715 Market Ave. NW
Canton, OH 44702
452-0665 x. 238

W9-BIP-969

# PRAYER
## FOR A CHILD

# BY RACHEL FIELD
PICTURES BY ELIZABETH ORTON JONES

**Aladdin Paperbacks**

*Aladdin Paperbacks*
*An imprint of Simon & Schuster*
*Children's Publishing Division*
*1230 Avenue of the Americas*
*New York, NY 10020*
*Copyright © 1941, 1944 by Simon & Schuster, Inc.*
*Text copyright renewed 1969 by Arthur S. Pederson*
*Illustrations copyright renewed 1972 by Elizabeth Orton Jones*
*All rights reserved including the right of reproduction*
*in whole or in part in any form.*
*First Aladdin Paperbacks edition, 1973*
*Also available in a hardcover edition from Simon & Schuster Books for*
*Young Readers*
*Library of Congress catalog card number: 84-70991*
*ISBN 0-02-043070-1*

PRINTED IN HONG KONG

*20   19   18   17   16   15   14   13*

FOR HANNAH

# PRAYER FOR A CHILD

Bless this milk and bless this bread.
Bless this soft and waiting bed
Where I presently shall be
Wrapped in sweet security.
Through the darkness, through the night
Let no danger come to fright
My sleep till morning once again
Beckons at the window pane.
Bless the toys whose shapes I know,
The shoes that take me to and fro
Up and down and everywhere.
Bless my little painted chair.
Bless the lamplight, bless the fire,
Bless the hands that never tire
In their loving care of me.
Bless my friends and family.
Bless my Father and my Mother
And keep us close to one another.
Bless other children, far and near,
And keep them safe and free from fear.
So let me sleep and let me wake
In peace and health, for Jesus' sake.

                              Amen.

less this milk and bless this bread

1791 9117

less this soft and waiting bed
Where I presently shall be
Wrapped in sweet security

hrough the darkness, through the night
Let no danger come to fright
My sleep till morning once again
Beckons at the window pane

less the toys whose shapes I know

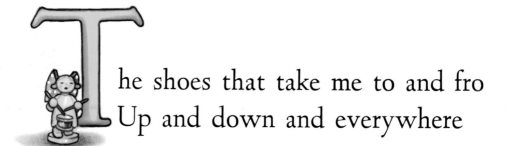

The shoes that take me to and fro
Up and down and everywhere

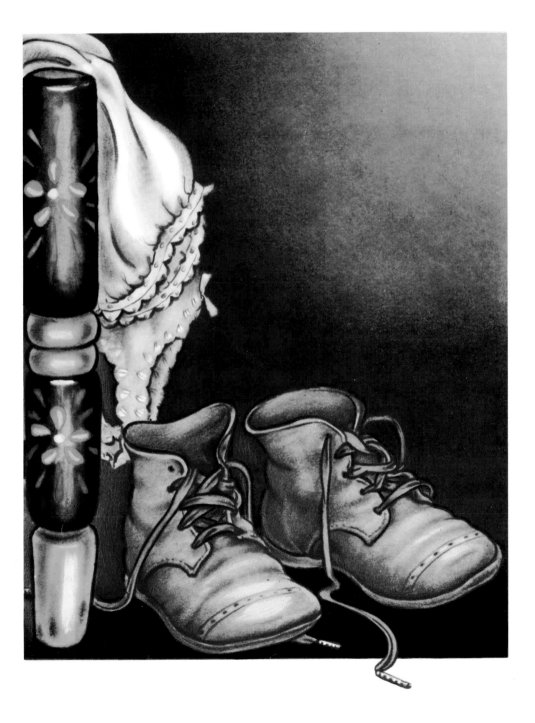

less my little painted chair

less the lamplight, bless the fire

less the hands that never tire
In their loving care of me

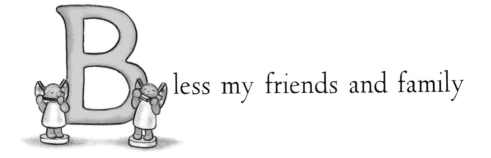

Bless my friends and family

less my Father and my Mother
And keep us close to one another

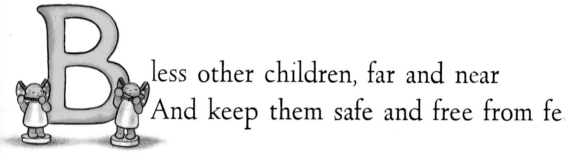

Bless other children, far and near
And keep them safe and free from fe

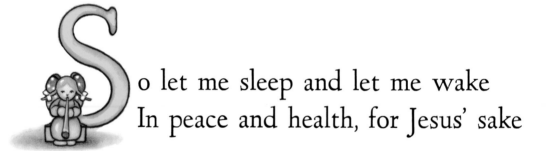

So let me sleep and let me wake
In peace and health, for Jesus' sake

men